Bottles
from the
Deep

Bottles
from the
Deep

Patent Medicines, Bitters, & Other Bottles from the Wreck of the Steamship *Republic*

by Ellen C. Gerth

Shipwreck Heritage Press

Books and other publications by Shipwreck Heritage Press celebrate the adventure of deep-sea exploration around the world.

Our books are available from fine bookstores everywhere. Visit our website for further information or to request a catalog. For other inquiries, contact us at Shipwreck Heritage Press, 1555 E. Flamingo Road, Las Vegas, Nevada 89119.

Shipwreck Heritage Press
www.lostgold.net

Publisher's Cataloging-In-Publication Data (prepared by the Donohue Group, Inc.)

Gerth, Ellen C.
    Bottles from the deep : patent medicines, bitters, & other bottles from the wreck of the steamship Republic / by Ellen C. Gerth. – 1st ed.

    p. : ill., maps ; cm.
    Includes bibliographical references and index.
    ISBN-13: 978-1-933034-07-2
    ISBN-10: 1-933034-07-6

1. Bottles. 2. *Republic* (Steamship) 3. Shipwrecks – North Atlantic Ocean. 4. Underwater archaeology – North Atlantic Ocean. 5. United States – History – Civil War, 1861–1865 – Antiquities. 6. Odyssey Marine Exploration (Firm) I. Title.

NK5440.B6 G47 2006
748.82

10 9 8 7 6 5 4 3 2
Printed in Canada

Cover design by Rebecca Hagen
Text design by Melissa Kronewitter

ACKNOWLEDGMENTS

To Odyssey co-founders, Greg Stemm and John Morris, I extend a huge thank you. It was both Greg and John who appreciated my passion for the history wrapped up in these bottles and suggested that I should write the book. A special thanks to George Becker for supporting me every step of the way, and to Roger Kurz for his infective encouragement and vast interest in bottles. Also, I am especially thankful to Neil Cunningham Dobson, Odyssey's archaeologist on the *Republic* project. Without Neil's thorough documentation of the wreck site, this book could not have been written.

In particular, I am also indebted to freelance researcher and bottle collector, Byron Dillé. Byron first introduced me to a great many of the colorful stories that brought these bottles to life, and for months thereafter, tirelessly answered all of my constant queries and provided me with exceptional follow-up research.

Thanks also to Odyssey's conservator, Wyatt Yeager and his dedicated staff, Alan Bosel and James Blackmon. Thanks to all of the other colleagues at Odyssey who have helped in so many ways to support this effort.

I am grateful to Philip Martin, our editor, whose experience and wisdom guided me through the process. Thank you to photographer George Salmon for treating each bottle as a work of art and to Odyssey designer Melissa Kronewitter for jumping into the project with enthusiasm. To my parents, Ina and Sam Gross, thank you for reading all of the copy and offering your editorial insight. And last, I thank my husband Dave, who understands my fervor, forgives my long hours, and has never stopped supporting me.

Ellen Gerth
June 2006

Foreword

When John Morris and I bought our first research vessel and entered the shipwreck business over 20 years ago, it was our love of the sea and all things nautical that drew us inexorably into the world of deep-ocean exploration. Little did we know that our passion would lead to finding hundreds of shipwrecks and creation of a company that would bring the world's best deep-ocean technology together with the most qualified and brightest technicians and explorers from all corners of the globe. One of the most significant projects that has resulted from the fusion of talent and technology was the archaeological excavation of the SS *Republic*, a side-wheel steamship lost in a fierce hurricane over 100 miles off the coast of Georgia in 1865. The project was not only a technical and financial success, but also provided a stunning time capsule of commerce immediately after the close of the Civil War.

As bottles came to the surface during the excavation, we were overwhelmed with the variety of commercial glassware and other containers that our robot gently manipulated from resting places 1,700 feet deep. Each bottle had a story to tell – of tonics, crackpot cures, spices, and hair restoratives. It was up to Odyssey's research team and other experts in the field to tease the data and tales from these unique pieces.

While the artifacts from the *Republic* belong to Odyssey's shareholders – and to those collectors that have purchased them, we strongly believe that the knowledge belongs to everyone. I am delighted that this book provides an opportunity to share the data we have accumulated – along with some amazing stories that provide a stunning historical overview of the times as told by the collection of more than 6,000 individual bottles, representing more than 175 types, recovered from the site.

Ellen Gerth wrote *Bottles from the Deep* to provide insight into each product, its maker, and its unique history – creating, in effect, a well-documented historical context for the use and consumption of many varieties of popular 19th-century bottled goods. As our research continued, Odyssey learned that these bottles comprise perhaps the largest and most diverse collection of its kind, representing a distinct moment in post–Civil War American history.

This publication is not meant to be a complete documentation of the entire SS *Republic* bottle collection recovered from the deep, and it only summarizes the related research and archaeological data that has been compiled to date. However, we hope this general historical overview of some of our more interesting bottles will help draw new audiences to the amazing collection and encourage a growing interest in the field of deep-ocean archaeology.

Our team is committed to conducting thorough archaeological research on the shipwreck sites we excavate. This book's appendix on the marine archaeological investigations features some of the data relevant to the discovery of the bottles and their dispersal on the site. Complete archaeological reports as published can be obtained by contacting Odyssey at www.shipwreck.net.

Greg Stemm, Co-founder
Odyssey Marine Exploration

A Note on Bottle Colors

A range of color terms exists in the world of bottle scholarship and study, making the objective naming of colors an inexact science. Also, there is at times a degree of color variation in the bottles themselves from one example to the next. In addition, bottle colors appear different depending on lighting methods used by photographers. We have made every effort to document and present these SS Republic samples accurately, but actual bottle colors are best viewed by direct examination.

Table of Contents

SS *Republic* **1853-1865**

INTRODUCTION

On July 25, 2003, an indistinct image appeared on a monitor screen. The weary search team from Odyssey Marine Exploration made another mark on their chart. They were surveying a vast section of the Atlantic, 100 miles off the coast of Georgia. Behind their research vessel, the R/V *Odyssey*, they were towing a side-scan "fish" – a sonar device shaped like a torpedo that uses sound waves to image the ocean floor.

This newest site with its curious echo was 1,700 feet below the surface, a mere dot in the deep sea. The sonar technicians were not convinced; it could be another false reading, one of many encountered as they had worked their way across a huge search area of nearly 1,000 square miles, week after week, month after month.

Was this enigmatic shadow on the sea floor the wreck they were looking for? As soon as they were able, the research vessel returned to the spot so the team could spend two days taking detailed sonar runs past the target.

With mounting excitement, the side-scan technicians realized the emerging image looked a lot like their target. When they calculated the wreck's size, it matched the known dimensions of the Civil War–era steamship *Republic* within a foot. After years of searching, had they found their ship on the deep Atlantic floor?

The SS *Republic* was a side-wheel paddle-steamer that had departed New York harbor in October 1865, just a few months after the end of the Civil War. The ship was bound for New Orleans, headed down the Atlantic coast to round the Florida peninsula into the Gulf of Mexico. Along with some 80 passengers and crew, its shipment included a remarkable cargo: a reported $400,000 in "specie" (gold and silver coins). In its hold, the ship also carried other goods sorely needed in New Orleans, a city once the cosmopolitan jewel of the South, now depleted by years of war and Union occupation.

But steaming south past Cape Hatteras, North Carolina, the *Republic* encountered rising seas and gusty winds. By the morning of October 24, 1865, the weather had become "a perfect hurricane" in the words of the captain, a relentless storm that tossed the side-wheel steamship about like a toy.

Pummeled by great waves, the vessel, which had seen service during the Civil War in the Gulf and on the Mississippi, sprang a leak. As walls of water smashed into the ship, her boilers failed and her paddlewheels stopped turning. The waves tore away her paddle-boxes, then ripped the pilothouse from the deck.

When the auxiliary pump finally quit, water filled the entire lower deck and the captain was forced to give the order to abandon ship. Quickly, passengers and crew climbed into four lifeboats and onto a crude raft and cast off. Within moments, after being battered for more than two days by the great storm, the ship disappeared beneath the waves and sank into the cold depths of the Atlantic.

The lifeboats were picked up in the following days, scattered across the high seas but with no loss of life, and the survivors were taken to Charleston and nearby ports. Those on the precarious makeshift raft were less fortunate; of almost twenty men originally aboard, only two survived their week-long ordeal.

The steamship's cargo, including many barrels of gold and silver coin, was considered lost forever. The last location of the side-wheel steamship when she sank after her two-day battle with the tempest was a mystery.

Now, 138 years later, Odyssey Marine Exploration, specialists in deep-sea marine exploration and shipwreck investigation, had found a promising wreck site on the sea floor, one-third of a mile deep, far beyond the reach of human divers.

The Odyssey team returned in the autumn with a larger ship, the *Odyssey Explorer*, equipped with a powerful remotely operated vehicle (ROV): a robotic submersible named *Zeus*.

The 251-foot-long deep-ocean archaeological platform, the Odyssey Explorer, *works over the site of the SS Republic wreck.*

Soon after arriving on the site, *Zeus* was lowered by a crane into the water and slowly disappeared into the deep blue waters, connected to the mother ship above by a coaxial cable. With video cameras and powerful lights, the ROV approached the wreck site

Odyssey's eight-ton remotely operated vehicle (ROV), Zeus, completed 262 dives to explore and excavate the SS Republic wreck site, recovering more than 51,000 gold and silver coins and thousands of other artifacts.

on the ocean floor, revealing the remains of a side-wheel steamship, sitting upright on the sea floor. The bow area was shattered from the impact after her long descent from the surface. Much of the hull had collapsed, leaving piles of shattered decking around the machinery and fittings of a mid–19th century steamship.

As *Zeus* maneuvered across the site, the video screens in the *Odyssey Explorer's* control rooms revealed an amazing variety of artifacts. Around the wreck could be seen piles of patent-medicine bottles, cases of inkwells, heaps of porcelain dishes, and stacked window-glass panes. There were bolts of silk and cotton cloth and bottles filled with preserved fruit. Religious items lay strewn about – ceramic angels and porcelain candlesticks. It was a snapshot of a world of goods lost just after the end of the Civil War.

On October 9, during an archaeological survey dive, the ROV team spotted a ship's bell lying in the sand. When the large bronze object was brought to the surface, the letters etched on it confirmed the wrecked ship was indeed the SS *Republic*.

By November, as the team finished mapping and photographing the site, the first coins were discovered: $10 and $20 gold pieces called eagles and double eagles. Many were from the 1850s and early 1860s, some were dated as early as the 1830s. Soon they found another surprise: great quantities of silver half-dollars. The recovery would eventually yield more than 51,000 coins, many in outstanding condition. Professional appraisers thought the coins might be worth as much as $75 million at retail values to collectors.

Equally fascinating, though, in historical terms, were the other objects recovered, approximately 14,000 of them, each one painstakingly mapped, videotaped, and carefully brought to the surface. Included were thousands of bottles, a huge cargo of glass containers that had been stored in the ship's aft and forward holds. Their shapes and sizes reflect a rich, diverse heritage of bottled goods in use around the time of the Civil War.

More than 6,000 bottles were recovered from the shipwreck site and the surrounding debris field. Many of the bottles were removed from the remains of wooden packing crates, which after years of saltwater exposure, abrasion from the strong Gulf Stream currents, and attacks from wood-boring creatures were far too deteriorated to recover. Often the crates were so degraded, like wet cardboard, that the dividers crumbled and disintegrated when the bottles were carefully lifted, one by one, by a soft limpet suction tool attached to a mechanical arm of *Zeus*.

The artifacts were placed gently in plastic containers with compartments, and then slowly brought to the surface where they were immediately examined on the ship by Odyssey's own research staff, including a project archaeologist.

The enormous quantity of bottles excavated from SS *Republic* wreck site is significant as an archaeological and historical resource. As a collection, they represent an extraordinary grouping of 1865 glass, one of the largest ever found. They tell us much about the manufacturing and technology of the day, and provide insight into how the bottles and their contents were used during the post–Civil War era.

Amazingly, most of the bottles were found unbroken. Many retained their original corks, often pushed inward by the great water pressure at the depth of 1,700 feet. A number of the bottles, however, still hold remnants of the contents they once carried. When the ship departed New York City, it seems to have been shipping mostly bottled goods, packed with varied products desired in New Orleans after the war's end. In 1865, with all major glassworks located in the North, the Northern states were the primary producers of commercial bottled goods.

It is possible that some bottles may have been shipped empty as a consignment to a Southern producer. It is also likely that a few of the bottles, especially those found in smaller quantities, were not part of the cargo but instead belonged to individual passengers or the crew.

The excavation and recovery of the bottles followed careful archaeological standards and practices. The positions of bottles were systematically documented by a database log that recorded all activities performed by the ROV *Zeus* during each dive. Video footage and still photographs further documented the recovery of each individual artifact.

Lying on the ocean floor under one of the ship's portholes, a Champagne-style bottle shares its space with a small fish.

Once the bottles were brought to the deck of the *Odyssey Explorer* in recovery baskets and containers, the archaeologist began a more detailed recording of each specimen. Onboard at a "first aid" conservation facility, the bottles were sorted by type and any marine growth was detached. Most sediments inside the bottles were removed, but samples with intriguing contents were left intact for further study.

After measurements and descriptions were recorded, each specimen was given a unique catalog number. More photography followed, then the bottles were packed for transfer to a land-based conservation laboratory. There, after 138 years hidden on the deep-ocean floor, the new life of the bottles began to unfold as additional research shed light on their extraordinary past.

Intriguing stories began to take shape as each bottle type was researched. Little-known facts emerged about the people who produced and promoted these goods,

A bottle of gooseberries is being recovered by the limpet attached to the ROV's manipulator arm.

as well as the consumers who needed them, purchased them, and believed in the efficacy of the products.

Each specimen, mouth-blown into a mold, is a work of art in itself. The entire collection together exhibits an impressive array of colors, spanning the full spectrum of shades and hues produced in glass at this time. The silent stories these many bottles tell reveal a remarkable past. They speak to a time when anything could be bottled and sold, when manufacturers swindled the public with outrageous claims, and when early victories of prohibition fever had lost momentum.

In October of 1865, the states were reunited; battlefields had fallen silent. The young country, only 89 years old, was attempting to recover from the crippling effects of the terrible four-year Civil War. It was the dawn of a new era, one that would have tremendous impact on Americans.

When Odyssey's skilled team of archaeologists, technicians, conservators, and researchers discovered the steamship *Republic* on the Atlantic seabed 1,700 feet deep, they had not expected that their long and patient journey would lead them to such a unique 19th-century time capsule. The ship's treasure of specie was spectacular.

An extraordinary amount of gold and silver coin was found, worth many millions of dollars.

But also recovered from the depths of the Gulf Stream was this other surprising wealth: thousands of bottles – bitters and inks, preserves and perfumes, and a plethora of patent medicines claiming extravagant healing qualities.

This booklet offers a glimpse of the rich assortment of bottles recovered from the 1865 wreck of the *Republic*, now brought to the surface and restored to view after a long, silent rest in the deep Atlantic.

An ornately patterned bottle rests on the Atlantic floor.

PATENT MEDICINES

Dubbed the Golden Age of Quackery, the 19th century was an era in which snake oil, worm pills, invigorators, and elixirs emerged on the market as sure cures for any and all afflictions. "Patent medicine" is the generic term given to these various compounds, sold under many colorful names and even more colorful claims.

In fact, these dubious medicines, today often referred to as "nostrums," were typically not patented but were instead often trademarked. Shrewd entrepreneurs marketed secret remedies registered under 20-year trademarks that were easily renewed. With a lack of federal drug controls, virtually anything could be sold without prescription – and without disclosing the contents. Proclaiming outrageous healing results, these magical formulas promised to cure everything from coughs, fevers, and constipation to all manner of disease, including cancer and diabetes.

The boom in patent medicines was fueled in part by a dramatic increase in newspapers. In 1800, there were only some 20 daily papers in existence. By 1860, the number had grown to 4,000, of which almost 400 were dailies.

With cheaper paper and larger steam-powered presses, tabloid-style papers were marketed to the common people. A vulnerable class of readers became the target of the nostrum promoter, who used the media and other creative ploys (calendars, trade cards, almanacs, etc.) to spread his mostly spurious health gospel. A survey of newspaper advertising in 1858 turned up over 1,500 patent-medicine names.

Dr. McMunn's Elixir of Opium

America in the 19th century has been called a "Dope Fiend's Paradise." Opium, morphine, heroin, and pharmaceutical preparations containing them were as accessible as aspirin is today. Most of the opium consumed in the United States was legally imported, but poppies were also grown lawfully on America's soil. Farmers in Vermont, New Hampshire, and Connecticut cultivated poppies, as did growers in Florida, Louisiana, and California. In Arizona, it was reported that ten acres of poppy fields could yield 1,200 pounds of opium.

Many opportunists profited from American's fixation with opiates. A host of products were advertised in newspapers and magazines and on billboards as "pain-killers," "cough mixtures," "women's friends," "consumption cures," and so on.

One such nostrum introduced around 1835 was Dr. John B. McMunn's Elixir of Opium. Soon after, ads for the product flooded newspapers and medical journals, all guaranteeing that McMunn's formula was not habit-forming. Bottles of the narcotic-laced formula were labeled as the "Pure and Essential Extract of the Native Drug" and was "Superior to Morphine." The remedy was said to alleviate a slew of maladies from ordinary pain to "Nervous Excitement," "Hysteria," and "Morbid Irritability of Mind and Body." By 1859, the Folembray glass works in France was producing millions of bottles annually for the sale of McMunn's Elixir alone, a testament to its tremendous popularity.

According to the 1846 American Journal of Pharmacy, Dr. McMunn's Elixir was "a preparation much in vogue" to which "wine has been added in sufficient quantity to insure its preservation." By 1864, plain alcohol had replaced the wine. (H: 4⅛")

During the Civil War, opiates became the pain killer of choice for thousands of injured soldiers. Opium pills, morphine rubbed into the wound, and later morphine by injection were in common use. The surgeons' reliance on these battlefield narcotics created a generation of post-war addicts, both North and South. Patent medicines such as McMunn's Elixir of Opium surely found a ready market among these survivors.

Many of the patent medicines recovered from the SS Republic once contained harmful narcotics, including Dr. McMunn's Elixir of Opium.

Mrs. Winslow's Soothing Syrup

The children's market was especially profitable for patent-medicine purveyors. With limited health care and high infant mortality, hope for an ill child was often purchased in the form of a small bottle – which frequently contained some sort of narcotic. One of the most famous was Mrs. Winslow's Soothing Syrup, a morphine-based formula bottled as a remedy for infant's "teething sickness." It was first formulated in 1835 by Mrs. Charlotte N. Winslow, a nurse who had treated children for almost 30 years. Her son-in-law, Jeremiah Curtis, and a partner, Benjamin A. Perkins, began marketing her recipe in 1849.

Mrs. Winslow's preparation enjoyed enormous success. Advertisements encouraged concerned mothers to use the syrup for their teething infants. "It Soothes the Child, Softens the Gums, Allays all Pain, Cures Wind and Colic, and is the Best Remedy for Diarrhea." The makers bragged that their product "relieves little sufferers at once, produces natural, quiet sleep by freeing the child from pain, and the little cherub awakes bright as a button."

Tragically, the popularity of this and similar morphine-laced products resulted in widespread drug addiction among children. Numerous infant deaths from overdoses were reported in newspapers. It was not until the Pure Food and Drug Act of 1906 that more stringent steps were taken to prevent the manufacture and sale of harmful children's nostrums.

As recommended on the backside of the trade card, "Mrs. Winslow's Soothing Syrup should always be used by Children Teething."

Mrs. Winslow's Domestic Receipt Book for 1865 *(above)* *claimed her soothing syrup "has been used with never-failing* *success in thousands of cases." (H: 4¾")*

Ayer's Cherry Pectoral

Child deaths were a scourge of the 19th century, and parents rich or poor were often helpless in the face of fatal infections and diseases that took away beloved children. Ayer's Cherry Pectoral was one of the popular products that claimed to cure dreaded childhood afflictions such as whooping cough, influenza, and consumption, as well as all diseases of the throat and lungs.

Advertising scare tactics played upon the fears of worried mothers. Ayer's trade cards delivered dire warnings to the conscientious caretaker "that every hour of delay in the effective treatment of such maladies is dangerous and may be fatal." They promoted the "curative virtues" of Ayer's Cherry Pectoral which, when taken promptly, was "the most reliable medicine that can be procured." Its effects "are magical and multitudes are annually preserved from serious illness by its timely and faithful use."

The Cherry Pectoral's "magic" was, in fact, due to its narcotic component, an

Advertised as "a Safe, Pleasant and Reliable Family Medicine," Ayer's Cherry Pectoral was one of the thousands of patent medicines that contained harmful opiates. (H: 7¼")

opium derivative which at the time was a legal ingredient. Opium preparations qualified as medicines and were available without restrictions. In particular, laudanum, a solution of opium and alcohol, was a favorite and was prescribed for various ailments including colds, meningitis, and cardiac disease.

The "genius" behind the Cherry Pectoral was James Cook Ayer. In 1841, at the age of 22, he bought Jacob Robbins' Apothecary in Lowell, Massachusetts, a shop where he had once clerked. Soon after, Ayer launched his Cherry Pectoral, followed by his Cathartic Pills, both of which were found among the *Republic*'s cargo of nostrum bottles.

Ayer's Cathartic Pills

Over 40 small rectangular bottles recovered from the SS *Republic* had once contained another of Ayer's remedies – his Cathartic Pills. Each bottle bears the embossed name of the product and its maker. At least one sample still holds the original small pills, remarkably undamaged.

Trade cards from the 19th century for Ayer's Cathartic Pills claimed that they contained only the purest vegetable ingredients, and noted they were coated with sugar to enhance their taste. The small tablets were designed to cure a host of ailments from flatulency, dizziness, and foul stomach to rheumatism, liver disorders, and kidney

Pea-sized tablets were packaged in this small bottle of Ayer's Pills, sold as a remedy for countless ailments including "Eruptions and Skin Diseases." (H: 2")

complaints. They were also touted as the best remedy for constipation and diarrhea.

The pills were first sold locally in wooden boxes from Ayer's apothecary shop in Lowell, Massachusetts. They were later packed in sealed glass vials for export to hot and damp climates. For decades before the war, such products were frequently advertised in the Southern press, promoted especially to deal with illnesses common to slaves. With the country at peace in October 1865, Southern cities were once again a promising market for patent medicines produced in Northern states.

Ayer's line of family remedies amassed the one-time apothecary clerk a vast fortune. By the early 1870s, his facility was producing over 600,000 doses of his preparations daily. His popular Cherry Pectoral even received global acclaim, shipped in special "ornate boxes" to foreign dignitaries.

When James Cook Ayer retired in the early 1870s, he had acquired an enormous fortune from his patent medicines. The Ayer Company was still going strong into the 1940s; its Pectoral and Pills had been available to the consumer for nearly 100 years.

The backside of this trade card for Ayer's pills noted that they are a "Universal Favorite."

30

H.T. Helmbold's Genuine Fluid Extracts

"Who has not heard of Buchu?" inquired one agent. "Why, this magic word adorns every dead wall, fence, rock and telegraph pole from the Atlantic to the Pacific." In the decades after the Civil War, painted patent-medicine slogans appeared on rocks, walls, trees, and private sheds and fences. These displays were often enormous and installed with disregard for property rights.

One of the most audacious was a self-described "doctor," Henry T. Helmbold, who introduced his Extract of Buchu in 1850. An eccentric man, Helmbold's marketing campaign extended along the entire route of the newly completed Union Pacific Railroad.

The leaves of the buchu plant, a small woody shrub, had long been used in South Africa by indigenous peoples as a traditional medicine. By 1840, the herb was officially recognized in America's pharmacopoeia for irritations of the bladder and urethra and for disease of the prostate.

Retail druggist Henry Helmbold (above) first introduced his Genuine Fluid Extracts in Philadalphia. Ads claimed it was "the anchor of hope to the physician." (H: 6½")

31

But Helmbold's recipe, labeled "Genuine Fluid Extracts," was a watered-down concoction of buchu with cubebs, licorice, caramel, molasses, peppermint – and, of course, alcohol. It was advertised as "a Specific Remedy" for an implausible laundry list of ailments: General Debility, Mental and Physical Depression, Imbecility, and Confused Ideas. Also on the list: Hysteria, Diseases of the Bladder and Kidneys, Emaciation, Constipation, Epilepsy, and Paralysis.

With descriptive treatises on the horrors caused by "excesses in married life, early indiscretion, or self abuse" – all of which, of course, his miraculous formula could remedy – the "doctor" realized great profits. Prone to excessiveness, Helmbold moved his Philadelphia establishment to New York. There, he constructed a $250,000 "Temple of Pharmacy," dubbed the most "Buchuful" structure on Broadway. It featured marble floors, perfume- and soda-dispensing fountains, floor-to-ceiling mirrors, and tweeting canary birds.

Underneath this facade of grandeur, Helmbold started to drink in excess, and was said to be "often crazy drunk." Over time, he deteriorated and was confined no less than seven times to an asylum, with intermittent recovery and relapses. In 1892, the inventor of "Genuine Fluid Extracts" died in his 66th year at his New Jersey seaside residence, where he had once entertained famous dignitaries, including President Ulysses S. Grant.

Mexican Mustang Liniment

"For the Outward Ailments of Man or Beast," Mexican Mustang Liniment was introduced in 1825 by George W. Westbrook of St. Louis, Missouri. The salve was said to cure over 30 ailments, including sprains, strains, burns, scalds, colds, sore throats, and lameness. Many of the claims were outrageously bold. One ad

"For man or beast," Mexican Mustang Liniment was said to cure harness sores and shoe boils, among dozens of ailments. (H: 4")

declared: "Use Mustang Liniment and you will be all right in a day or two, so will your horse."

Some 25 years later, Dr. A.G. Bragg had become a well-known agent for Westbrook's formula. On the heels of the Mexican War (1846–48), Bragg popularized the product with melodramatic claims that the nostrum was "oil from the burning mountains of Mexico." In fact, the pungent liniment was a mixture of bottled crude petroleum, ammonia, water, and brandy.

One of the most effective ads for the product was the sensational large mural that Bragg had painted on the exterior of his St. Louis drugstore, capturing the dramatic events of April 18, 1847, when the Americans stormed the Mexican position at Cerro Gordo, opening the road to Mexico City. The prominent name of the liniment was accompanied by life-sized depictions of the Mexican general, Santa Anna, and his troops fleeing the victorious Americans. The general's artificial cork-and-leather leg was depicted lying where it had fallen on the battlefield. An erupting volcano in the background completed the enormous painting.

Located near the "Gateway to the West," the mural was seen by thousands of people passing by on their way to the California goldfields on wagon, horse, or foot. News of the liniment spread, and it became a popular bestseller. Sometime in the late 1850s, the creator of the liniment, Westbrook, sold his business to Demas Barnes and Co. Barnes was building his patent-medicine empire, and the 30-plus bottles of Mexican Mustang Liniment recovered from the *Republic* wreck site bear his name embossed on the product.

Stephen Sweet's Infallible Liniment

Dr. Stephen Sweet's Infallible Liniment was championed as "The Great External Remedy for rheumatism, gout, neuralgia, lumbago, stiff neck and joints, sprains, bruises, cuts and wounds, piles, headache and all rheumatic and nervous disorders."

The "infallible" recipe, prepared by the "famous bone-setter" of Lebanon, Connecticut, would also cure toothache, quinsy, sore throat, sores, ulcers and even frosted feet.

The word *liniment* is derived from the latin word *linere*, which means to annoint. Many liniments allegedly contained snake oil, considered a universal panacea. From this folklore came the term "snake-oil salesman," one who peddles a quack cure with smooth, false promises.

Ads for Dr. Stephen Sweet's Infallible Liniment proclaimed sensational cures from toothache to frosted feet. (H: 5¼")

B.L. Fahnestock's Vermifuge

The South offered a lucrative market for patent medicines. Poverty was pervasive, with common diseases caused by an inadequate diet. The warm, humid climate was conducive to a high incidence of malaria and yellow fever. Rural areas in particular were plagued with diseases linked to improper sanitation, such as those caused by the intestinal parasite, hookworm, which thrives in the loamy and sandy soils of the South. Rural children, often shoeless, were easily infected. After the Civil War, half of the Southern children were afflicted with hookworm disease.

To combat this invasive parasite and other intestinal worms, an army of "cures" flooded the market. Worthless preparations and products were sold to a vulnerable, unsophisticated crowd. "Vermifuge" became a common household term as hundreds of products to expulse worms were pitched to the public.

Benjamin A. Fahnestock of Pittsburgh, Pennsylvania, introduced his brand of vermifuge in 1830, heralded as the "The Safest and Most Effective Remedy for Worms in Children and Adults, that has ever been discovered." His product was so popular that it spawned many imitators, including one introduced in 1858 – prepared and marketed in the same small cylindrical bottles – by "B.L. Fahnestock & Co."

The two specimens of Vermifuge recovered from the *Republic* wreck site were indeed the copycat versions made by B.L., not B.A. It is not known if the imitation formula was similar to Benjamin's original recipe, said to contain tincture of myrrh, drachm,

B.L. Fahnestock's Vermifuge was touted as a remedy for intestinal worms. (H: 4")

oils of wormseed and anise, croton, and turpentine.

This vile concoction, to be swallowed by the teaspoonful, must have caused further misery to the poor young souls already suffering from those nasty worms.

Dr. McLane's American Worm Specific

Intestinal parasites, a serious 19th-century affliction, worked to the advantage of the shrewd patent-medicine man, including Dr. C. McLane who introduced his popular worm-killer in 1844. When the *Republic* steamed from New York in 1865, the Pittsburgh doctor had already been dead for ten years, but his American Worm Specific continued to flourish under John and Cochrane Fleming of the Fleming Brothers company. The partners acquired McLane's company in 1855 and continued to market his formula under its original name.

As testament to its widespread availability, the *New Orleans Times Picayune* published a notice on July 8, 1855, that McLane's "celebrated Vermifuge can now be had at all respectable drug stores in the United States and Canada." It was also noted for sale "by all respectable druggist[s]" in New Orleans.

The 1855 announcement touting McLane's product seems to have been submitted by Scovil & Mead, "wholesale agents" for the "Southern States" whose business was located on 111 Chartres Street, New Orleans.

Dr. C. McLane of Pittsburgh formulated American Worm Specific to address the common intestinal affliction caused by poor sanitation. (H: 3¼")

Perhaps the *Republic*'s cargo of McLane's American Worm Specific, shipped a decade later in 1865, was a consignment for one of those same "respectable" New Orleanian druggists.

Color lithograph features McLane's Vermifuge (American Worm Specific), sold at Fleming's Southern Patent Medicine Warehouse in New Orleans.

Doctor Marshall's Snuff

In the 15th century, during Columbus' second voyage of discovery, American Indians were seen sniffing a mysterious powder: tobacco. The entrepreneurial explorer introduced this snuff-taking habit to Europe, and the pungent leaf later became a popular crop for European colonists farming in America.

Snuff's potential as a patent medicine was not overlooked by the clever nostrum maker. One such proprietor was Dr. Benjamin Marshall of New York, who first marketed his product in the early 1830s. Ads touted it as a cure for "Nearly All Common Diseases of the Head, Except Wrong-Headedness."

More than 100 empty snuff bottles were recovered from the SS *Republic* wreck site. Most are square or rectangular, without embossment, in green and brown glass, their paper labels washed away.

But several samples of clear glass are unmistakably Marshall's. With the doctor's name embossed on one side, the dozen or so vials are surviving specimens of this once-popular cold remedy.

Much the vogue in the 19th century, snuff was often sold in a plain bottle like this squat example (upper left), then transferred to small decorative dispensers carried on the person. (H: 4¼")

Dr. Marshall's snuff (lower right) was advertised as a cure for "Common Diseases of the Head, Except Wrong-Headedness." (H: 3¼")

BITTERS

The consumption of "bitters" for digestive ailments – loss of appetite, indigestion, and weakness of the stomach – is many centuries old. Home-brewed recipes from the 17th and 18th centuries involved steeping roots or herbs in brandy or spirits for several days. Water instead could have been used, but alcohol was the preferred medium in which to soak the roots and extract their medicinal virtues. The result was a disagreeable bitter taste, but that did not deter consumption. Originally, bitters were meant to be taken by the teaspoonful, a few drops swallowed now and then to stimulate the digestion.

By the middle of the 19th century, bitters-taking had grown in popularity, and claims for its curative attributes extended well beyond the digestive tract. For thousands of Americans, a dose of bitters had become a daily habit – and this dose now was often larger, taken by the shot-glass or small cordial glass.

Under the guise of its herbal ingredients, the alcoholic content of bitters could be overlooked by the emerging temperance movement. With a free conscience, avid bitters consumers enjoyed their cocktail not just before dinner, but often before breakfast and lunch as well. Not surprisingly, a wave of medicinal bitters flooded the 19th-century market to satisfy this pervasive bitters addiction.

Dr. J. Hostetter's Stomach Bitters

During the second half of the 1800s, the Temperance Movement gained momentum. As states North and South enacted prohibition laws, Americans developed a strong thirst for bitters. Amid the early rumblings of this era, Dr. J. Hostetter's Stomach Bitters emerged on the market in 1853, sold as a medicinal tonic. Its alcohol component was promoted as a vital ingredient, needed to "preserve the medicinal properties of vegetable extracts in a fluid state."

Hostetter insisted that his secret formula gained its potency from its herbal ingredients – that the inclusion of whiskey, tipping the scales at a whopping 47 percent alcohol, was simply the best vehicle to deliver the remedy.

"Just one bottle creates an appetite, forces off impure bile and purifies the system," read an 1856 newspaper ad. But if one was good, two were better. "Two bottles cures bad livers and lends strength and cheerfulness."

The concoction was first formulated by Dr. Jacob Hostetter, a prominent Pennsylvania physician who for years had prescribed to his patients his home-brewed tonic for various stomach and digestive ailments. It was not the

Hostetter's Stomach Bitters, with its high alcoholic content, was advertised as a "medicinal cordial . . . suited to greatly mitigate the infirmities of age" and to restrain "the natural physical decay attendant upon advancing years." (H: 9")

The 1876 Hostetter & Smith Almanac (following page) included pages of testimony promoting Hostetter's Stomach Bitters as a "Sovereign Health Preservative."

doctor, but his eldest son, David, who popularized the recipe and established the Hostetter venture. In partnership with childhood friend George W. Smith, David patented the Stomach Bitters and sold it under the trademark "Hostetter & Smith."

In pursuit of health, thousands of Americans, ailing or otherwise, sought relief in Hostetter's potent brew, believing that a dose a day would keep one healthy and in good spirits.

The Civil War offered nostrum-makers a new opportunity. Hostetter jumped on the bandwagon, claiming that his bitters were "a positive protective against the fatal maladies of the Southern swamps, and the poisonous tendency of the impure rivers and bayous." Consumption of the product increased when the War Department authorized its distribution to the Union Army. Train car-loads of Hostetter's Stomach Bitters were delivered to appreciative troops, who knew it as "The Soldier's Safeguard."

When the fighting was over, the Hostetter appeal remained strong. Over 6,000 bottles of Hostetter's Stomach Bitters were sold daily in the United States and abroad. Its popularity continued to soar into the early 20th century. But with the passage of the 1906 Pure Food and Drug Act, the alcohol content was cut to 25 percent. During Prohibition, its herbal content was increased and its taste became less tolerable to the average consumer.

Drake's Plantation Bitters

Sold as medicine rather than as liquor, bitters were not subject to tax and were immensely popular in the second half of the 19th century. Their curative attributes permitted the respectable man to satiate his desire for strong drink without incurring condemnation from the temperance union – or from his neighbor.

The bitters trade reached new heights from 1860–1880 as thousands of brands were introduced on the market, competing for a share of the multi-million-dollar business.

Drake's Plantation Bitters was one of those brands. Sold in a distinctive bottle with log-cabin sides and three-tiered roof thatching, its design was patented in 1862. Drakes's was one of the first of more than 40 cabin-shaped bitters bottles produced by various makers during the patent-medicine era.

The formula was first manufactured and marketed by Patrick Henry Drake in partnership with fellow New Yorker, Demas Barnes.

In 1867, Drake established the P.H. Drake Company with himself as sole proprieter.

Drake's Gratuitous Medical Annual *for 1871–1872 (above left) cautioned to beware of "Counterfeits and Imitations" and to avoid bottles "purporting to be Plantation Bitters" but not "verified by the name, in full, on the bottle and label. . . ."*

Drake's Plantation Bitters was proclaimed a "wonderful vegetable restorative" and "the sheet anchor of the feeble and debilitated." (H: 10")

The famous recipe, "a wonderful vegetable restorative," contained a mixture of herbs, laced with St. Croix rum from the Caribbean.

The potent formula – over 38% alcohol – claimed to cure every disease known to mankind.

"Why is it that Plantation Bitters outsells all others?" began one announcement in Drake's popular yearly almanac, followed by a long list of medicinal claims: "it promotes digestion," "purifies the blood," "puts new life into a lazy liver," and "corrects all the defects in the gastric functions," including "nervous constipation," to mention but a few.

Competition in the bitters market was intense. Drake and his competitors issued large amounts of promotional literature attesting to the curative powers of their products. Testimonials were fabricated from "cured" users, including President Grover Cleveland's wife.

Like so many patent-medicine men, Drake could not resist the urge to spread his therapeutic message across America's

The distinctive bottles of Drake's Plantation Bitters feature hues of yellow olive, amber, and yellow topaz. (H: 10")

Lediard's Morning Call was one of many bitters brands that appealed to the American consumer. (H: 10½")

open spaces. An entire mountainside forest was chopped down by Drake's agents so that 400-foot-high letters forming the words "Plantation Bitters" could be read by passengers on the Pennsylvania Railroad.

By the 1880s, however, the bitters industry was under attack by the medical community. Reform campaigns strove to abolish the blatantly false claims of the proprietary formulas.

With the Pure Food and Drug Act of 1906, the government cracked down on the sale of all questionable medicinal products, and the bitters trade was mortally wounded.

The excavation of the SS *Republic* yielded a huge cargo of bottles embossed with Drake's Plantation Bitters. Over 150 samples were recovered, most in varying shades of amber.

Lediard's Morning Call

As consumers in the mid-1800s developed a fondness for alcohol-spiked herbal remedies, thousands of bitters brands inundated the market. The profits attracted many enterprising merchants, such as Charles Lediard of New

York, who sought to enter the fray and grab a piece of the action.

From 1860–1880, the New York City directory listed Lediard as a liquor merchant and bitters manufacturer. Lediard sold a variety of bitters brands, including his Morning Call and OK Plantation Bitters.

Advertised as a "tonic and invigorating cordial bitter," less than a dozen bottles of Lediard's Morning Call were excavated from the site.

Lediard's OK Plantation Bitters

While Lediard's Morning Call bottles were few, even fewer of his distinctive OK Plantation bottles were found.

Lediard originated this tri-cornered bottle design to market his Plantation Bitters recipe. The bottles were produced in varying shades of amber, ranging from lighter golden tones to darker purple-reds.

Its unique three-sided log-cabin design is rather rare, which suggests that it was not one of Lediard's more successful products. Its scarcity today makes the OK Plantation Bitters bottle a prized specimen for modern-day collectors.

New York liquor merchant Charles Lediard sold his OK Plantation Bitters in this unusual three-sided bottle, prized by collectors today. (H: 11")

Moffat's Phoenix Bitters

John Moffat introduced his Phoenix Bitters about 1834. The New York City merchant widely advertised his "Universal Cure" and reached markets both South and West. An 1840 newspaper advertisement claimed that, when taken at night, his remedy would "promote insensitive perspiration and relieve the system of febrile action and feculent obstructions as to produce delightful convalescence in the morning."

After 1862, Moffat's Phoenix Bitters became the property of John's son, William, although the bottles continued to be embossed with the senior Moffat's name. The bottles were sold for $1 or $2, depending on size. By 1845, the company had introduced at least one other remedy, Moffat's Vegetable Life Pills, along with an almanac, a popular advertising medium to promote patent medicines. *Moffat's Agricultural Almanac* for 1845 featured "certificates of remarkable cures performed by Moffat's remedies."

Moffat's Phoenix Bitters warned: "Beware of Counterfeits and Imitations . . . both in New York and the Canadas, and per consequence, the public at large have been the great sufferers." (H: 6¼")

Three $1 bottles of Moffat's Phoenix Bitters, now empty, were salvaged from the wreck of the *Republic*. Were they the few surviving specimens of a larger shipment – or the favorite brand of a bitters drinker on board as passenger or crew?

Boerhave's Holland Bitters

Boerhave's Holland Bitters were sold by Benjamin Page Jr. & Company of Pittsburgh. The company first offered the product in 1856, promoting it widely with colorful advertising.

The *North Carolina Standard* of July 8, 1857, declared that Boerhave's Holland Bitters "finds its way directly to the seat of life, thrilling and quickening every nerve and raising up the drooping spirit."

When Page entered the U.S. Navy in 1862, he apparently sold his interest in the business, leaving no record of subsequent owners. However, it seems that this liquor-laced remedy continued to enjoy some appeal through the end of the Civil War.

Only two bottles of Boerhave's Holland Bitters were salvaged from the wreck of the *Republic*. Perhaps these two samples, now empty of their contents, were drained by a nervous passenger during the storm-tossed voyage of October 1865.

Boerhave's Holland Bitters was an alcohol-rich recipe for "raising up the drooping spirit." (H: 7½")

Dr. Hoofland's German Bitters

C.M. Jackson was yet another Philadelphia bitters distributor. He began to sell Dr. Hoofland's German Bitters around 1850. The product had been introduced much earlier, its formula developed by a German doctor. According to the 1890 *Hoofland's Almanac*, the product was "the happy result of intelligent research, coupled with the extensive practice of Dr. Christoph Wilhelm Hueflin of Gena, Germany."

As noted on the embossed bottles, Hoofland's bitters were marketed as a remedy for "Dyspepsia" and "Liver Complaint." An ad proclaiming the benefits of Hoofland's put it simply: "It is for him [the potential customer] to say whether he will continue to endure a living death or to put himself in a position to render life enjoyable."

By 1863, the product was sold to Charles Evans and R.S. Jones, and a decade later, the proprietors of Hoofland's German Bitters were Johnson, Holloway and Company of Philadelphia.

Only a dozen bottles of Dr. Hoofland's German Bitters were recovered from the Republic wreck site, a small sampling compared to other bitters brands recovered, notably Hostetter's and Drake's. (H: 8")

Lady's Leg Bottles

Some 15 uniquely shaped "Lady's Leg" bottles were recovered from the shipwreck, all without embossment or a maker's paper label. Also referred to as a "swell neck," the bottle acquired the name Lady's Leg from the distinctive contour of its neck, which may have been designed for easy gripping.

These curious specimens may have once contained the famous "aromatic" Boker's Bitters, advertised as "unequalled for their medicinal properties and their fineness as a cordial." Boker's was produced by J.F. and J. Boker of New York. They may have been the inventors of this odd bottle shape (or perhaps were the first to use it in the United States for a consumer product).

Boker's cardamom-tinged formula was a favorite ingredient in 19th-century cocktail recipes, including those concocted by Jerry Thomas, a famous New York bartender of the period. Thomas' creations received acclaim in his treatise "How to Mix Drinks, or the Bon-Vivant's Companion," first published in 1862.

The Bartender is said to have died in 1885 at the age of 55, the victim of apoplexy. Boker's Bitters didn't last much longer – perhaps overtaken by competitors. "Beware of Counterfeits and Imitations" reads one familiar warning in the *New York Weekly-Tribune* of April 30, 1879. It is possible that the Lady's Leg bottles recovered from the *Republic* were indeed Boker fakes.

The "Lady's Leg" bottle shape was often used for bitters. (H: 12")

WINE, BEER, & SPIRITS

Originally, wine was stored in wooden casks, ceramic amphorae, or jugs. By the first century A.D., Roman glass, often in the form of square bottles, carried wines, spirits, and other beverages. However, for centuries afterward, the use of glass bottles for alcoholic beverages was still uncommon. The earliest wine and spirits bottles found in the American colonies were typically English-made imports; there were no significant American producers until the late 18th century. But the frequency of wine bottles and their fragments found at historic U.S. sites is testimony to the massive consumption of alcoholic beverages throughout the centuries.

As early as 1750, efforts were made in both England and America to reduce excessive drinking of wine, beer, ale, and other intoxicating spirits, whether fermented or distilled. By the 1820s, people in the United States were drinking on the average seven gallons of pure alcohol per person each year. Religious and political leaders made repeated efforts to discourage excessive drunkenness, which was seen at the time as a national curse.

In the mid–19th century, Abraham Lincoln was among those concerned. He said that intoxicating liquor was "used by everybody, repudiated by nobody." He added that it presented itself in society "like the Egyptian angel of death, commissioned to slay if not the first, the fairest born in every family."

As the relationship between drunkenness and the incidence of crime, poverty, and violence became more apparent, many concluded that the only way to protect society from this menace was to abolish the "drunkard-making business." The state of Maine passed the first prohibition law in 1851, prohibiting the manufacture and sale of "spiritous or intoxicating liquors" not intended for medical or mechanical purposes. Within four years, 13 of the 31 states had instituted similar laws, and the annual per-capita consumption of absolute alcohol fell to about two gallons.

However, the early prohibition fervor was soon overshadowed by the political crisis preceding the American Civil War. Many of the early state laws were repealed, modified, or simply ignored. The widespread manufacture and sale of anything alcoholic resumed with few restraints.

After the Civil War, as the population increased rapidly, soon there were more than 100,000 saloons throughout the country. By 1870, there was approximately one drinking institution for every 400 man, woman, or child, all competing for the drinkers' wages. It is quite likely that the considerable quantity of wine, beer, and liquors shipped aboard the *Republic* just months following the end of the war were intended to help restock the shelves of New Orleans' bustling saloons.

Wine Bottles

The cargo of wine bottles on the *Republic* included the prevailing types popular in the early 19th century: hock, Bordeaux, and champagne. These distinctive bottle shapes originated in Europe and are still produced today with only subtle variations.

All of the bottles recovered from the *Republic* wreck site are missing their original paper labels, and since wine bottles are rarely embossed, little can be gleaned about the products' names or makers.

In the 19th century, wine bottles were produced in limited colors, usually in shades of olive green, amber, or less often, aqua or colorless glass. Most feature a distinctive indentation or "kick-up" in the base, not common on other bottle types.

Hock-style

The term "hock" is believed to be an English derivative of the word Hochheim, a German village that was the first exporter of Rhine wines to England. Hock bottles typically contained red or white Rhine or Mosel wines. Over 100 tall, slender hock-shaped bottles, in varying shades of light and dark amber, were recovered from the shipwreck. This bottle type is also sometimes called a "Rhine."

Bordeaux-style

The "Bordeaux" bottle is typically a tall body with almost vertically parallel sides, and a moderately steep shoulder and neck. The steep indentation or "kick-up" in the base is distinctly visible through the glass. A large number of transparent green or colorless Bordeaux wine bottles (also referred to as claret, sauterne, or Cabernet Sauvignon) were discovered at the site, in two sizes. Most still contain their cork stoppers, now eroded

The hock-style wine bottle (left) has a long tapered neck. In contrast, the Bordeaux bottle (above) has a taller body. (Left H: 13⅞", right H: 11½")

with age, forced into the bottles by the increased pressure as the ship sank.

Similar Bordeaux bottles, in nearly pristine condition, were found on the steamboat *Bertrand*, which sank in the Missouri River in April 1865, the same year as the *Republic*'s last voyage. The *Bertrand* samples suggest that the *Republic* bottles likewise may have been imported from France.

It is possible that the *Republic* bottles were produced in the United States. American manufacturers were producing the claret bottle type as early as 1800. An 1819 ad for Thomas Pears & Company announced the firm had "obtained a complete set of workmen from . . . France" and that its new factory would produce claret bottles "of the same kind and quality of the imported." An 1831 New England Glass Company ad also noted that their claret bottles were a "correct imitation of the French."

Champagne-style

The characteristic "champagne-style" bottle has vertically parallel sides, with a distinctive long sloping shoulder that merges seamlessly into the bottle's neck. It also features thick glass, as the bottle was designed to withstand the internal pressures of carbonation and also helped prevent spoilage from heat. Examples from the 19th century typically have a deep indentation in the base, the "kick-up" or "punt," which is less defined in bottles of the 20th century.

The term "champagne" refers to sparkling wines from the Champagne region of France. But champagne-style bottles are found in surprising numbers in historic archaeological sites of the mid-1800s. This bottle type has been excavated, for example, in large quantities at Civil War–era Western Army forts where most soldiers would not have been drinking champagne. Likely the bottles were also used for less expensive products such as wine or beer. This might explain the large shipment carried aboard the SS *Republic*.

The cargo of champagne bottles retrieved from the shipwreck site included two sizes. More than 100 examples of a small version (10 inches high, much like today's split) were recovered. The larger 12-inch-high variety was found in fewer numbers.

In most cases, the cork was compressed and forced into the bottle during the 1,700-foot descent to the deep-ocean floor, allowing sea water to replace the contents. Remarkably, however, some bottles still had their corks intact. Extra care was taken when handling these bottles so the contents did not explode.

A few of these classic green bottles contained a whitish-yellow emulsified substance – not a wine product, but instead with oil-like characteristics. One sample had the appearance and texture of cottage cheese; another was more like butter. The bottles also had a rotting organic odor. It is possible that the substance may have been a vegetable oil, perhaps even olive oil. It was not uncommon in the 19th century to reuse bottles for various foods or other products, much like our use of modern-day Tupperware.

Champagne-style bottles were often used for bottling wine and beer, which may explain the prevalence of these bottles in 19th-century historic sites. (H: 12⅛")

Beer and Ale Bottles

In the 1860s, beer and ale bottles were round in cross section (inherently a strong shape), and made of a thick glass to withstand the pressures of carbonation as well as to survive extensive handling. Often these bottles were reused – refilled and sold again. Given the frequent re-use, some beer bottlers embossed their bottles with bold statements such as "This Bottle is Never Sold," to assure customers that the contents were the original ones.

Most beer and ale bottles produced before 1870 were in shades of green, olive green, amber, cobalt blue, or aqua, as well as black glass. The hundreds of examples recovered from the SS *Republic* exhibit some of these color variants, with a few especially rare samples featuring an unusual peacock blue.

Many of the beer bottles in the ship's huge inventory are the typical early-export beer shape common from 1860 to 1880. It was produced in two sizes, the common small bottle, which was about a pint, and a larger quart size.

This sturdy bottle once contained beer or ale. The cork stopper that sealed its contents is now inside the bottle. (H: 8¼")

Black Glass Bottles

In the first half of the 17th century, glass blowers in England began making black glass. American glassmakers soon learned the process and were producing such bottles by the late 18th century.

The term "black glass" refers to shades of dark green, dark amber, deep purple, or brown. Often the glass is so dense that the color appears black, the result of impurities in the batch or the density of the ingredients.

The most common agent producing the dark color is iron oxide. The oxide darkens the glass and strengthens it as well, reducing breakage. The dark color also inhibits exposure to light which better preserves the contents, whether beer, ale, porter, or cider.

American breweries used these types of bottles in the mid–19th century, filling them with their brands of ale, lager, or stout, then adding their distinctive brewery labels. (Left H: 10", right H: 8¾")

Case Gin Bottles

The square bottle was first produced in the Roman era. Its early proportions were squat, evolving over time into a taller bottle type that emerged later in the 16th century, most likely in Germany. Square bottles were depicted in many paintings by Dutch, Flemish, and Spanish masters. The bottles were also made in 17th-century England, and it seems that liquor in square bottles was being shipped to the American colonies at the end of that century. Square vessels may have also been produced in the mid–17th century American glassworks of Salem, New Amsterdam, and New York.

The square bottles fit easily into a wooden packing case. By the 18th century, the term "case bottle" was being used. Further developments produced bottles with slanted sides that tapered from top to bottom, forming a base that was narrower than the shoulder. Such bottles were often filled with gin, and by the 19th century, the name "gin bottle" or "case gin" was common.

The several green samples found at the *Republic* wreck site have neither distillers' stamps nor trademark seals. The bottles are unembossed, so little is known of their specific makers or contents.

The square "case gin" bottle was convenient for shipping in wooden cases. (H: 9¾")

Square Spirits Bottles

As the 1800s progressed, the short-necked tall square bottle continued to be produced in a non-tapered form. Its classic shape was used for a wide assortment of products from high-alcohol medicinal bitters to sarsaparilla. Schnapps (brandies distilled from fermented fruit) were common contents. The vessels were also used by the apothecary and the chemist.

Over 400 of these distinctive bottles were recovered from the SS *Republic*. Most are in shades of green that, when illuminated from behind, glow with brilliant hues of olive, yellow, grey, and blue. The excavation also produced some amber samples.

With their makers' labels long gone and lacking any embossed text on their sides, the identity of this portion of the bottled cargo is forever uncertain. However, considering the large quantity of embossed bitters bottles also found at the site, it is likely that these square bottles, too, were filled with some brew of bitters so popular in the middle of the 19th century.

Without a maker's label or embossment, the identity of these bottles remains obscure, but such bottles often held bitters or schnapps. (H: 9⅞")

FOOD BOTTLES

The mid–19th century experienced what historians have called the second phase of the Industrial Revolution. This era saw the development of steam-powered ships and railways and, significantly, the mass production of consumer goods. With mechanization came vast improvements in food production, preservation, storage, and shipping.

The impact on everyday life was enormous. As society evolved from an agrarian-based model to a more industrial one, fewer families grew their own foods. More people relied upon prepared products. Population increases in the city meant bottled goods like peaches, pickles, peppers, flavorings, relish, and sauces needed to be produced and packaged in greater quantity.

This legacy of bottled food goods is often seen through archaeological excavation of land sites, including 19th-century dumps and privies. Such sites generally show an accumulation over many years – refuse found in heaps of discarded, left-over, unwanted materials.

In contrast, the specimens recovered from the SS *Republic* provide an exact glimpse of one distinct and significant moment in history: a cargo of select goods carried aboard a steamship at sea, soon after the end of the Civil War, heading South to aid New Orleans after years of economic isolation.

Cathedral Pickle Bottles

The cathedral-patterned bottle was an American invention. Typically, three sides had fancy arches framing ornately embossed panels. The fourth side was left smooth for a product label. By selling their products in elaborate bottles, American merchants hoped to convince the consumer that their preserved goods were superior to imported English brands in plainer bottles.

The SS *Republic* carried an impressive cargo of what collectors today call "Cathedral Pickle" bottles. Pickles were not the only fare preserved in such bottles, but pickled vegetables were a key staple in the 1800s, the equivalent to our modern salad. Over 150 of these utilitarian bottles were recovered from the shipwreck site.

Many are in subtle shades of aquamarine, while others exhibit deeper hues, such as apple or forest green. Some of these containers hold the eroded remnants of their original cork stoppers, which may at one time have been covered with coal tar and a plain foil seal.

Cathedral Pickle bottles with elaborate designs stored a variety of preserved foods important in the 19th-century American diet. (H: 11")

The bottles were made in two-piece molds, and were found on the wreck site in four sizes. Cathedral Pickle bottles were often made of relatively thin glass, making their survival from the ship's two-day battle with a hurricane and their subsequent descent to the deep-sea floor remarkable.

The original contents and paper labels of the SS *Republic* samples have long since vanished, but a similar find of bottles from the same era suggests what these decorative containers may have once held.

The year the SS *Republic* sank off the coast of Georgia, the steamboat *Bertrand* sank in the Missouri River with an estimated 250 tons of cargo. The bulk was bottled goods, discovered more than a century later in nearly pristine condition. Many of the *Bertrand* bottles were the Cathedral Pickle type, still with their paper labels and original food contents: mixed vegetables, peppers, honey, plum tomatoes, and a hodgepodge of pickles with spices. A few jars even held the exotic tart and sweet tamarind fruit, testament to the diversity of foodstuffs stored in Cathedral Pickle bottles of the era.

Many of the examples found on the Republic *site feature an uncommon cross-hatch pattern. (Left H: 9", right H: 7½")*

Lea & Perrins Worcestershire Sauce

Lea & Perrins Worcestershire Sauce has been popular around the world for over a century. According to legend, the sauce originated in India and was a favorite of Lord Sandys, an English nobleman from the county of Worcester. Upon returning home in 1835 from his travels, Sandys approached two chemists, John Lea and William Perrins, who owned a thriving apothecary. Asked if they would replicate a recipe Sandys had acquired in India, the men kindly concurred. Their finished product, however, was a disappointment, a fiery hot mixture that the chemists banished to their cellar.

Some two years later, Lea and Perrins stumbled across their concoction and decided to taste it again. To their surprise, the recipe had mellowed. Now delightfully pungent and aromatic, it had matured much like a fine wine. Its new flavor so impressed the chemists that they immediately bought the recipe from Lord Sandys and in 1838 launched the sauce commercially.

Within a year or two, the bottled sauce was imported into the U.S. by John Duncan & Sons of New York. By 1849, the condiment was being sold west of the Mississippi as thousands of gold seekers made their way to California's gold fields.

Lea & Perrins Worcestershire Sauce gained its flavor from a long mellowing process. (H: 8¾")

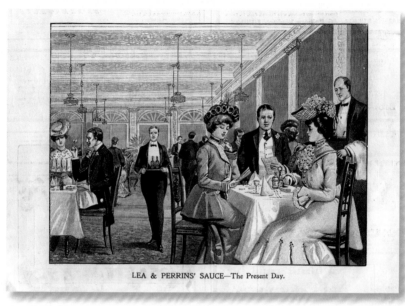

LEA & PERRINS' SAUCE—The Present Day.

Lea & Perrins famous sauce was popular in dining cars, restaurants, hotel dining rooms, and on passenger ships, as seen in this ad circa 1900.

In 1865, when the SS *Republic* departed from New York harbor, it carried a large cargo of two sizes of Lea & Perrins Worcestershire Sauce bottles.

More than 250 bottles were recovered from the wreck site. All bear the original Lea & Perrins embossment, which by the early 1920s was replaced by a paper label. The glass-and-cork stopper, found intact on almost half of the samples, was in use until 1957 when replaced by a screw cap.

Lord Ward's Worcestershire Sauce

The success of Lea & Perrins produced many imitators, typically sporting pretentious names such as "British Lion" or "Empress of India." One such imitation, believed to be of English origin, was Lord Ward's Worcestershire Sauce.

While today little is known of the maker, the product apparently had some customers in the United States in 1865. However, only a few of these bottles, embossed with the name Lord Ward's Worcestershire Sauce, were found at the wreck site, a paltry number in contrast to the huge shipment of Lea & Perrins more esteemed condiment.

Lord Ward's Sauce is one of the many Lea & Perrins imitators that appeared on the market in the mid-1800s. (H: 8")

Cathedral Pepper Sauce Bottles

Pepper sauces were an important staple in the 19th-century American diet, enjoyed for their distinctive flavor and for their ability to mask unpleasant tastes. They were commonly used to season meat that had spoiled due to a lack of cold storage. Small cylindrical bottles were often carried by Civil War soldiers of the North and South. The product was especially useful in hot and humid summers when unsavory meats were served on a regular basis.

Massachusetts was home in 1807 to the first known American bottled pepper sauces; the recipes were probably similar to earlier English ones. By 1859, a prominent Louisiana banker and legislator, Colonel Maunsell White, manufactured the first bottled hot sauce. A key ingredient was Tabasco chilies harvested on his own plantation. A friend, Edmund McIlhenny, later marketed the spicy formula in used cologne bottles and by 1870, had obtained a patent on Tabasco hot pepper sauce, the second oldest U.S. food patent.

Many 19th-century American pepper sauces were sold in cathedral-style bottles. More than 150 such bottles were recovered from the wreck of the SS *Republic*. In varying shades of aquamarine – some with deeper tints of blue, others are more green – they typify the common designs of square and six-sided cathedral patterns. At least a half dozen of the bottles still hold some remnants of their original contents: well-preserved red or green chili peppers, floating in a murky liquid, now contaminated with sea water and ocean deposits.

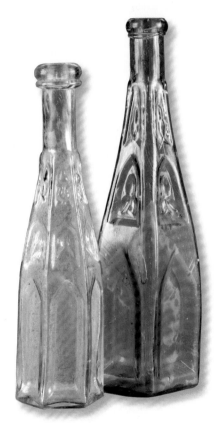

Pepper sauces were often bottled in fancy cathedral-style jars. Several samples recovered from the seabed still boast their well-preserved chili peppers. (Left H: 8¾", right H: 10")

Preserve Bottles

A number of remarkable bottles recovered from the wreck still contain a fascinating assortment of fruits, now almost a century and a half old.

Pineapple, peaches, blueberries, gooseberries, and rhubarb were discovered, packed in cork-sealed preserve bottles with distinctive rounded shoulders and cylindrical necks. The bottles no longer have paper labels, and their wooden packing crates have long since eroded away, making it impossible to identify company names or other clues as to the origins of these found treasures.

Still, the pieces of fruit speak their own language, suggesting a fondness for fruit compotes, pies, pickled delights, and other hearty and nutritious edibles that formed an important portion of the everyday diet of Americans in the mid-1860s.

Bottles containing peaches and other tasty fruits were shipped aboard the Republic, *perhaps part of the ship's provisions for passengers. (H: 11¾")*

A. Kemp Preserves

Throughout history, people have sought better methods to preserve food. A major breakthrough came in the era of Napoleon Bonaparte. His soldiers' diet of mostly salt-preserved foods was vitamin C deficient, leading to outbreaks of scurvy. Napoleon offered a reward of 12,000 francs to the person who could devise a safe and dependable method of food preservation.

After years of tests, French chemist Nicolas Appert found that food could be preserved if sealed in airtight glass jars and then boiled. Appert submitted his invention in 1809 and won the prize, personally awarded by Napoleon.

Appert's process involved filling thick, large-mouthed glass bottles with edibles, leaving air space at the top. Using a vise, the contents were tightly sealed with a cork, then the bottle was wrapped in canvas and dunked into boiling water.

The method spread swiftly across the Atlantic. By 1835, Aaron Kemp of New York was preserving meats with great success. From archaeological sites of the California Gold Rush, we know that Kemp's products were enjoyed as far west as San Francisco. Kemp joined George W. Day in 1862. Kemp, Day & Co. were listed as "Packers and Preservers of Meat, Poultry, Game, Fish, Fruits, Vegetables, Shell Fish, Pickles, etc."

The excavation of the SS *Republic* yielded over 160 jars embossed with A. Kemp's name. Most are empty, only their large corks inside. But two bottles, their corks still intact, are generously filled with ripe yellow pineapples, sliced and well conserved – a fine example of Kemp's preserving skills.

Now protected with a modern plastic cap, preserved chunks of pineapple were recovered from the Atlantic seabed, tightly sealed after more than 135 years. (H: 9¾")

Burnett's Vanilla Extract

The embossment on the Burnett bottle provides little information about the product it once contained. One side reads "Burnett" and the other side, "Boston." It seems likely that this bottle was once filled with Burnett's Vanilla Extract. According to ads, it was made from the "choicest" Vera Cruz vanilla beans. Burnett reportedly bought up half of the crop to ensure that he had an ample stock of the best beans.

Proclaiming the superiority of his beans, another Burnett ad boldly states that the use of his vanilla extract was not only "advisable" and "desired" but "almost necessary."

Joseph Burnett of Southborough, Massachusetts, was one of the few patent-medicine vendors of the era who actually received a degree in pharmacy. In 1840, Burnett joined Theodore Metcalf, a Boston dealer of drugs and toilet articles, later becoming a partner. Around 1847, Burnett opened his own business and began to make flavoring extracts.

When the *Republic* sank in 1865, Burnett had been selling his popular vanilla extract for almost two decades. Perhaps the dozen bottles

Joseph Burnett's Vanilla Extract was said to have been made from the "choicest" vanilla beans grown in Vera Cruz, Mexico. (H: 7")

of Burnett's extract retrieved from the wreck site came from the ship's pantry, where it may have been used to flavor the passengers' desserts.

Clarke & White Mineral Water

The mineral springs of Saratoga, New York, had long been revered by local Native American tribes. The Iroquois called one such site, the High Rock Spring, the "medicine spring of the Great Spirit."

Tucked between the Hudson and Mohawk rivers, the Saratoga region was first settled for its wild game, prized for its rich fur. The superior quality of the local fur was attributed in part to the area's saline springs. After the American Revolution, word spread about the region's abundant natural resources and wonderful waters.

Arriving in 1822 in Saratoga Springs, New York City soda-fountain owner John Clarke saw the commercial potential of the area's pure waters. He purchased land and established a venture bottling the mineral water. Experienced with carbonated beverages, he was the perfect person to promote the product. With partner Thomas Lynch, Clarke successfully marketed his bottled water across the country and Europe.

When John Clarke purchased several springs in Saratoga, New York, and a bottling plant nearby, he became the first to market bottled mineral water. (H: 7½")

An astute businessman, Clarke made his mineral water available free to the locals. And to ensure an ample supply, he did not bottle it during the summer months, the peak season for visitors. Instead, pitchers, jugs, and kegs were filled generously by "dipper boys" in attendance at the spring. A posted sign affirmed Clarke's generosity and marketing savvy: "Any remuneration given to the boys will be exclusively for their benefit. John Clarke."

In 1828, Clarke married the widow Eliza White who had purchased the High Rock Spring. Together the couple formed a company, Clarke & White, to bottle their Saratoga mineral waters. After Clarke's death in 1846, their children managed the business for some years.

Mustard Barrels

Mustard has been a widely cultivated plant around the world for centuries. Its origins date back at least 3,000 years to Ancient Egypt. The Romans used it as a condiment and seasoning as well as for medicine. They carried the seed to Gaul, and by the 9th century, French monasteries were making a profit selling mustard preparations.

Mustard was believed to cure sundry ailments including hysteria, snakebites, and even the bubonic plague. Mustard has also been used therapeutically to relieve sore muscles and for bouts of congestion.

When the SS *Republic* sank, mustard was an indispensable enhancement to the 19th-century diet. It was often used to disguise the taste of meat and other foods turned rancid from lack of refrigeration. Mustard added a zesty flavor to egg dishes, salads, casseroles, and vegetables.

The sizeable cargo of glass mustard barrels recovered from the shipwreck – among the largest quantity by type, numbering well over 250 – is proof that this pungent condiment was a sought-after staple and would surely have been valued in post–Civil War New Orleans.

The clear-glass mustard barrels traveling aboard the *Republic* all feature a similar ribbed pattern. The jars may have once held either dry or prepared mustard, both of which were sold in these distinctive containers.

A few unique mustard bottles from the shipwreck site have a yellow-orange tarnish, perhaps the century-old stain of their original contents, but more likely the result of contact with a rusting metal object. (H: 5")

HAIR PRODUCTS & BEAUTY AIDS

Treatments and therapies to improve one's body for beauty or health had long been pitched by quack practitioners. Until the early 20th century, there were no laws in the United States regulating the claims and efficacy of medical products. Beauty remedies were advertised heavily in newspapers, on trade cards, and in yearly almanacs offered in drugstores and local shops.

The outdoor landscape also provided vast marketing opportunities, as did traveling medicine shows, featuring theatrical pitchmen. The entertaining barker seldom failed to draw a crowd, first in amusement, then in amazement at the miracles claimed. Soon, gullible customers were lining up to buy the cure-all that promised to hide all blemishes and attract passionate interest from members of the opposite sex.

Hair restorers, invigorators, and scores of miracle creams inundated the market, all competing for the attention of the balding consumer. The shrewd medicine man was always thinking of new ways to promote his product, often offering pseudo-scientific wisdom as a proven way to bolster any advertising campaign.

Hundreds of phony hair preparations flooded the 19th-century market. Despite their bold claims, none were likely to actually prevent hair loss or promote hair growth. Still, these popular products were marketed with astonishing success to those concerned with their physical appearance.

Perfume Bottles

Hundreds of glass perfume bottles were recovered from the SS *Republic*. Some still have their original glass stoppers and at least one still contains some liquid contents. Many of the bottles are unidentified, their makers' labels long since eroded away.

A few bear the embossed name of distinguished 19th-century perfumers, such as Lubin of Paris. Pierre-Francois Lubin established his Royale Street perfumery in 1798 and produced fragrances, lotions, powders, and toilet waters used by King George IV and the Emperor of Russia, among others. Pierre-Francois died in 1853 to be succeeded by a former apprentice.

A selection of American perfumes also graced the *Republic*, including more than 50 bottles credited to a maker named Edrehi. Unlike Lubin, whose fragrances can still be found today, little is known of the New York perfumery that Edrehi launched in 1862.

French perfumes by Lubin (above left) competed with perfumes by American makers such as I.D. Edrehi of New York (lower right) for sale to Southern belles on the plantations of Louisiana. (Left H: 4", right H: 4¼")

Edward Phalon's fragrances caught the public's attention with his elegant Bower of Perfume, featured in the Crystal Palace Exhibition at the New York World's Fair in 1853. Offering a line of hair products and perfumes, Phalon was joined by his son Henry in 1858. Their New York company became known as Phalon & Son's Perfumery, the name found on more than a dozen perfume bottles recovered from the wreck site.

Best known for his hair products, Edward Phalon also developed a line of perfumes in partnership with his son. (H: 4½")

PHALON'S BOWER OF PERFUME, IN THE CRYSTAL PALACE, NEW YORK.

"Phalon's Bower of Perfume" in New York's Crystal Palace at the 1853 World's Fair.

Murray & Lanman's Florida Water

Scattered on the seabed were also a handful of bottles that once contained Murray & Lanman's Florida Water, named for the peninsula once believed to be the source of the fabled Fountain of Youth.

Robert I. Murray of New York launched his cologne in 1808 and was joined in 1835 by David T. Lanman. The firm was known at first as Murray & Lanman, but soon the name changed to David T. Lanman and Co., then in 1861 to Lanman & Kemp. Still, the original name of the cologne was kept.

Murray & Lanman's Florida Water is still produced today, having thrived on the market for almost two centuries. A modern ad recommends using the cologne "like Holy Water for cleansings, good luck, and protection."

Advertised as the most delicate of all perfumes, Murray & Lanman's Florida Water was a popular cologne first introduced in 1808. (H: 9")

THE FLOWERS OF PARADISE.

Among the inhabitants of the lands of the far East there is a legend which tells of flowers that grow in Paradise eternally in bloom, the perfume of which, when once inhaled, insures perpetual happiness, filling the soul with such delight as human tongue can not describe; but here, in our favored section of the universe, we need not wait for entrance into Paradise before partaking of the enjoyments and pleasures afforded by the

Richest Floral Fragrance.

IN
MURRAY & LANMAN'S
Florida Water

we have all that is excellent in the breath of the rarest flowers, whether for richness, purity, delicacy, or durability, and besides these admirable qualities there are a host of virtues in its

HYGIENIC PROPERTIES

which were never even claimed for the flowers of Paradise.

The backside of this trade card for Murray & Lanman's Florida Water warned that "numberless imitations have been foisted upon the public; consumers should therefore beware of counterfeits. . . ."

THE GENUINE MURRAY & LANMAN FLORIDA WATER
The richest of all PERFUMES

Burnett's Cocoaine

Among the many claims of the nostrum maker was a promise to restore lost hair or prevent it from falling out. "The Inventors of Burnett's Cocoaine," testimonials claimed, relied on "pharmaceutical science" to produce "the most desirable [hair] preparation ever offered to the public."

Through "careful research and reiterated experiment," the makers discovered that coconut oil, with other "scientifically selected" ingredients, created the ideal compound to stimulate "healthy and vigorous hair growth."

When Joseph Burnett of Southborough, Massachusetts, named his "Cocoaine" in 1856, he may have intended to play off the public's attraction to the many cocaine-laced patent medicines being sold to treat other ailments. Burnett, however, stands out as one of the few proprietors to have been a fully qualified pharmacist, having graduated from the Worcester College of Pharmacy.

Burnett first went to work for Theodore Metcalf, a Boston dealer of drugs and toilet articles. In 1847, the young pharmacist opened his own apothecary in Boston. Ten years later, Burnett partnered with William G. Edmonds, and the business became Joseph Burnett & Co.

Made from coconut oil and 50 percent alcohol, Joseph Burnett's Cocoaine was labeled "A Perfect Hair Dressing." At just fifty cents a bottle in 1859, it was also promoted as "the best and the cheapest hair dressing in the world." (H: 7")

The company boasted a number of products including "Jonas Whitcomb's Asthma Remedy," a cologne water, flavoring extracts, a freckle remover, and its most lucrative preparation, Burnett's Cocoaine. This last item was one of the most popular hair treatments of the era.

More than 40 bottles of Burnett's prized hair formula were salvaged from the wreck site. Two of the bottles contain a clear liquid that may be the remnants of the original product.

Two 19th-century ads for Joseph Burnett's Cocoaine.

Phalon & Son's Chemical Hair Invigorator

Years before Burnett launched his famous Cocoaine, Edward Phalon had already captivated the public with his Chemical Hair Invigorator. The New York hairdresser and wigmaker introduced his hair treatment in the early 1840s at his elegant Franklin House establishment on Broadway Street. This richly embellished bathing and hair-cutting emporium boasted elaborately painted walls and Italian marble flooring, with "sumptuous" interior furnishings of rosewood and crimson velvet.

An 1849 advertisement for Phalon's Franklin House promoted his Chemical Hair Invigorator, said to "clear the pores, dissolve impurities and keep the hair moist. . . ."

Around 1858, Phalon was joined by son Henry and the company became Phalon & Son's Perfumery, offering an extensive line of perfumes, hair dyes, and even a Bear Oil.

Of the bottles of hair products found at the shipwreck site, over 70 were Phalon & Son's Chemical Hair Invigorator, recovered in two different sizes. All are embossed with the family name. Most are empty. A few select samples, however, still have their corks securely intact and display an oily substance inside, which may be the remains of Phalon's original potion.

Phalon & Son's miraculous Chemical Hair Invigorator was recommended to prevent hair "from turning gray, rendering it silky and glossy and preserving the hair through life." (H: 7")

Also among the *Republic*'s shipment of hair products were over 75 small vials that once contained Phalon's Magic Hair Dye, Nos. 1 and 2. The ingredients in these little rectangular bottles may have been a two-step hair-dye process, the results of which one can only speculate.

Barry's Tricopherous

The self-declared "Professor," Alexander C. Barry, was a New York wigmaker who had never actually received any academic degree.

Barry's Tricopherous for The Skin and Hair was nonetheless a popular product. The "Professor" claimed that his father established the Tricopherous formula in 1801, although this too may be another Barry tale. The product was first sold in the United States around 1842.

Ads for Barry's hair preparation included popular trade cards, typically featuring a beautiful woman with luxurious, long-flowing hair. The ads claimed the product was "guaranteed to restore the hair to bald heads and to make it grow thick, long and soft."

More than 80 bottles of Barry's famous Tricopherous were retrieved from the wreck site. They had once

Trade card from the 19th century promoting Barry's Tricopherous.

contained Barry's alcohol-based formula combined with some castor oil and other fragrant oils. The product's most active ingredient, though, was its one-percent tincture of cantharides.

Cantharides came from the dried, crushed bodies of the *Cantharis vesicatoria beetle*, also known as the blister beetle or Spanish fly. When threatened, the beetle produces a caustic irritant called cantharidin. The theory was that this substance would stimulate blood supply to the scalp, which in turn would promote hair-follicle growth.

Barry claimed that "if the pores of the scalp are clogged, or if the blood and other fluids do not circulate freely . . . the result is scurf, dandruff, shedding of the hair, grayness, dryness and harshness of the ligaments, and entire baldness. . . ."

"Stimulate the skin" he claimed, with Tricopherous, and "the torpid vessels, recovering their activity, will annihilate the disease."

Cantharidin, however, is today recognized as a toxic substance that can cause severe gastrointestinal disturbances if ingested, sometimes leading to convulsions, coma, and possible death. Still, Barry's formula was sold well into the 20th century. Even today, a search of the Internet yields sites selling modern versions of Barry's Tricopherous hair tonic, marketed as "based" on the original formula.

The cargo of hair products aboard the Republic *included many bottles of Barry's Tricopherous. (H: 6")*

Mrs. Allen's World's Hair Restorer

Mrs. Susan A. Allen, the wife of a New York City dentist, introduced this product around 1840. By 1854, she was selling it from her husband's Broome Street practice, the "Manufactory and Depot" for Mrs. Allen's World's Hair Restorer.

"Sold By Druggists Worldwide," her product enjoyed a global market with consumers in Canada, Great Britain, and on the island of Cuba.

Promotional material for Mrs. Allen's formula emphasizes in bold that it "Is Not A Hair Dye," but rather was designed to "Restore The Hair To Its Original Youthful Color." The recipe for this "Great Unequaled Preparation" contained a mixture of "sulphur, acetate of lead, glycerin, and flavored water" – hardly a concoction likely to enhance the beauty of hair.

The excavation of the *Republic* wreck yielded but three bottles of the hair restorer – rectangular with beveled corners, in a deep amethyst color. Were these samples part of a larger cargo of the formula? Or were they aboard the vessel in the luggage of a passenger or crew member?

Bold claims declared that with regular use, "you will not have a gray hair if you should attain the age of one hundred years." (H: 7 ¼")

Lyon's Kathairon for the Hair

"No one desiring a fine head of hair should fail to use it," claimed ads endorsing Lyon's Kathairon as a cure for baldness and gray hair. Promoted as "the most excellent and popular preparation for the hair ever made," the product was introduced by German-born Emanuel Thomas Lyon, an 1840s graduate of New Jersey's Princeton College.

After leaving college, Lyon began working as a chemist in New York City where he concocted several preparations, including his popular Kathairon.

Advertising in 1856 and 1857 claimed that nearly a million bottles of Kathairon had sold the previous years. Period ads featured testimonials of individuals documenting their return from baldness to a full head of hair. One such gentleman claimed that Lyon's remedy "has entirely restored my hair after baldness of six years."

Lyon died in 1858, just ten years after he had introduced his hair restorative. But his creation continued to thrive until the end of the 19th century. The cargo of Kathairon carried on board the *Republic* in 1865 had been prepared by wholesale druggist Demas Barnes, who was amassing a great fortune through his patent-medicine empire.

Lyon's Kathairon: "the most excellent and popular preparation for the hair ever made." (H: 6½")

Heimstreet's Inimitable Hair Restorative

The shipment of hair products salvaged from the *Republic* wreck site included two sterling samples of Heimstreet's Inimitable Hair Restorative, notable for its uniquely shaped octagonal bottle of cobalt blue.

Ads claimed Heimstreet's hair coloring "does not act as a dye, but stimulates the natural secretion of coloring at the roots and thus restores its natural color."

Charles Heimstreet was listed as a druggist in Troy, New York, from 1835 until his death in 1855. His brother Stephen joined the company in 1838 to manage the bottled-medicine line. By 1845, the business was called Heimstreet & Bigelow, and a few years later was assumed by William E. Hagan, a former clerk in Heimstreet's store.

At some point in the early 1860s, the New York wholesale druggist Demas Barnes became sole proprietor of Hagan's articles, including Heimstreet's original hair formula.

Heimstreet's Inimitable Hair Restorative "restores gray hair to the original color" and "imparts health and pleasantness to the head." (H: 6¾")

G.W. and J. Laird, Perfumers

The excavation of the *Republic* produced a handful of white milk-glass bottles. A few are embossed with the name J. Laird and at least one sample bears the name G.W. Laird.

According to the 1865 New York City directory, George W. Laird, located at 483 Broadway, was a "Perfumer & Importer of Human Hair" and a manufacturer of wigs, toupees, and braids.

Laird's inventory included "a large stock of hair, jewelry constantly on hand and made to order." James Laird was also listed in the directory at the same address – perhaps a father-and-son partnership.

A hole in one of the bottles reveals a hard, pink substance, the remains of the original product.

Priced at 75 cents a bottle, "Laird's Bloom of Youth" was touted as ideal for "Beautifying and Preserving the Complexion & Skin." (H: 4½")

T & M Bear Grease Pomade

Victorian hair care included the use of bear's grease, applied either with the hands or with a soft brush. Users were warned not to spread the oil too freely, as an over-oiled head of hair was both offensive and vulgar. They were also advised before going to bed to rub the hair with a piece of flannel to remove the excess oil and not spoil the pillow when they laid down their head.

As evidenced by the steamship *Republic*'s large cargo of hair products, post–Civil War New Orleans offered a ready market for a variety of hair preparations, including bear grease. Over 20 small green rectangular bottles embossed "T & M" on both sides were recovered from the shipwreck site, each having once contained Taylor and Moore's bear-grease pomade.

Alfred Taylor and James Moore were New York drug importers and distributors of a few medicinals, but their primary line was perfumery goods including their bear-grease formula.

At one time thought to be an ink bottle, the T & M bottle was later discovered to have contained bear-grease pomade, a popular hair-care product in the mid-1800s. (H: 2½")

INK BOTTLES

Commercial inks were available to some extent in 17th-century America. Colonists could buy liquid ink for government or business use and for writing books and keeping diaries. The most common form, though, for the average writer consisted of cakes, sticks of ink, or powder. The purchaser would then add water to make his own liquid ink. It was not until the 19th century that commercial liquid ink became more readily available.

In colonial times, containers for liquid ink were usually ceramic, pottery shipped from suppliers in England. However, by the 18th century, glass bottles were the container of choice. Although more easily broken than pottery, the glass permitted users to see the level of ink remaining. Later, when American manufacturers introduced their own inks, they were probably sold in both ceramic and glass bottles, since in 1800 there were only 8 glass houses. By 1832, however, there were 71 glassworks operating, more than half of them blowing bottles.

Soon, glass factories across the nation began producing ink bottles in varied shapes. The ideal design was attractive and had a stable base to avoid tipping over.

When the steamship *Republic* departed New York in October 1865 loaded with a large cargo of ink bottles, there were hundreds of glass factories, large and small, from New York to Virginia. Most produced utilitarian items such as window panes and bottles, with inkstands a standard production item.

Umbrella Inkstands

Inkstands remained out on a writing table or desk, so their visual appeal was important. The "umbrella" inkstand (also called a "paneled pyramid" or a "fluted cone stand") was a shape popular from the 1840s to the latter part of the century.

Intended for post–Civil War New Orleans, the inkstands aboard the *Republic* were perhaps headed for schools, including new ones established for the former slave population. Nearly 500 umbrella inkstands were recovered from the SS *Republic*. Most had eight panels and typically came in shades of aquamarine. Many, however, exhibit wonderful hues of green.

When placed in the light, the aqua samples can display the colors of the rainbow, refracting the sunlight – the result of long exposure to saltwater and its corrosive action on the glass. The ship also carried some specimens whose dark amethyst color is rare today in the collectors' market.

A handful of umbrella inkstands found at the site are an uncommon larger version with eight or twelve panels. They may have been intended for use by an artist or sign maker.

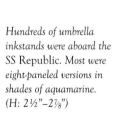

Hundreds of umbrella inkstands were aboard the SS Republic. Most were eight-paneled versions in shades of aquamarine. (H: 2½"–2⅞")

Conical Inkstands

By the 1840s, the slate and slate pencil were becoming obsolete, replaced by small ink bottles and pens in home and school. A common bottle was the "conical" inkstand, also called the "plain pyramid." Its production continued into the early 20th century.

The conical inkstand typically has a cone-shaped body that tapers upward to a short cylindrical neck. It was blown in a variety of colors. The excavation of the SS *Republic* has recovered more than 140 examples in clear or aqua glass. Several still contain the dried remnants of their original red ink clinging to the interior glass. One exceptional sample holds a red liquid, which may be the ink fluid now mixed with some sea water.

Most have a short narrow neck. Yet some of the conical inkstands retrieved from the site have no neck at all; they are also much smaller in size. These inkstands were ground down at the shoulder, featuring what is called a "ground-lip" finish. Such inkstands often had a metal crimped top with a hinged cap to cover the bottle's corked mouth. However, if so, one would expect to see some remains of the original metal affixed to the bottle. To date, none has been found.

Perhaps these small inkstands were designed to be part of a traveler's set, complete with paper, pens, ink, nibs, and a writing surface – the 19th-century equivalent of our modern laptop.

This unique sample of a conical inkstand (top) boasts its original liquid ink. The lower photo shows an inkstand with a "ground-lip" finish, lacking a neck. (Top H: 2½", bottom H: 1¼")

School House Inkstands

The SS *Republic* carried a large shipment of ink bottles for home and school use, but few of the specimens recovered from the site have a manufacturer's embossment. All are also lacking any original paper label which would have identified the ink maker.

Over thirty square inkstands were found among the cargo. With its boxy body and beveled roof-like corners, many bottle collectors call this distinctive shape a "cottage" or "school house" inkstand. Like other period inkstands, it was designed to be attractive, but is less elaborate than some examples produced in this era which feature well-defined windows, doors, and rooftops.

A few of the ship's cottage inkstands still hold their original reddish-purple writing fluid. Over the years, this has coagulated and settled to the bottom, with a pale red liquid filling the remainder of the bottle.

One unique specimen exhibits a bulging side and an irregular neck, defects that probably occurred during its manufacture. Given the costs of production and limited industry regulation, it was not uncommon in the 19th century to sell flawed merchandise.

When recovered from the seabed, this "school house" inkstand still contained its writing fluid, well over 135 years old. (H: 2½")

Guyot Inkstand

The modern ink industry is said to have begun in 1625 when the French government offered a chemist named Guyot a contract to manufacture a large amount of "gall" ink. Prepared from nut-shaped galls of oaks or other trees, gall ink is an Asiatic invention believed to have entered Europe through Arabia at the end of the 11th or early 12th century.

Guyot has been called "the father of the modern ink industry."

In 1865, when the *Republic* sank, more than two centuries after that first contract was issued in France, the Guyot company still flourished as makers of fine ink. More than a dozen square ink bottles were retrieved from the *Republic* wreck site, each embossed with the Guyot family name.

While any labels have long since washed away, many of these bottles still hold their original cork stopper, and at least one bears the stain of the original writing fluid.

These square ink bottles bear the embossment of the Guyot ink company, a firm that dates back to 17th-century France. (Left H: 2¾", right H: 2½")

Master Ink Bottles

In comparison to the small inkwell or decorative inkstand placed on the desk ready to receive a writer's dipped pen, the master ink bottle was a large container.

It was used to hold bulk ink, sometimes in a concentrated form to be diluted before using. These bottles, often with pouring spouts and produced in a variety of sizes, were then used to refill smaller inkwells.

In addition to its remarkable cargo of many inkstands, the SS *Republic* carried over two hundred "master inks." More than half are unembossed clear, amber, or green glass bottles, in several sizes. Most feature a pouring lip, distinctive to this bottle type and useful for the clean and efficient dispensing of fluid ink.

The lip on these master ink bottles was designed for easy pouring when refilling smaller containers. (H: 7½"–8")

J. Bourne & Son Stoneware

Larger quantities of ink could also be stored in stoneware containers such as these made by Joseph Bourne & Son's pottery of Derby, England. Over 90 of these master ink bottles, in three sizes, were recovered from the wreck site.

Each bears the stamp of the Bourne pottery, plus the mark of a London ink company, P. & J. Arnold, an ink-making firm dating back to 1724. The Arnolds' writing fluid was widely imported into the United States by the mid–19th century and could still be purchased into the 1940s.

The Bourne pottery, founded in 1809 by Joseph Bourne, is still in existence today. The fine clay from which this stoneware was made was discovered in 1806 during construction of a road in Derbyshire.

When William Bourne, a local entrepreneur, realized the clay's exceptional qualities, he acquired a piece of land and assigned his youngest son, Joseph, to run a business to produce salt-glazed pottery.

By throwing common salt into pottery kilns when the embers were hottest, the salt vapor combined with the surfaces of the pots to produce the shiny brown coating.

These salt-glazed stoneware bottles made by J. Bourne & Son's pottery contained P. & J. Arnold's fluid ink; both company names are stamped on the bottles. (Left H: 5¾", right H: 7¼")

APPENDIX A

Archaeological Notes

by Neil Cunningham Dobson, M.Litt. AIFA

In October 2003, Odyssey Marine Exploration of Tampa, Florida, commenced its deep-water archaeological investigation and artifact recovery of the side-wheel steamer SS *Republic*, lost in a hurricane on October 25, 1865. The shipwreck was discovered one hundred miles off the Georgia coast, in over 1,700 feet of water.

The wreck lies on the seabed in the strong currents of the Gulf Stream at a depth well beyond the normal diving range of an underwater archaeologist. Therefore, the investigation and excavation had to employ robotic submersible technology, similar to that used in other fields engaged in precision deep-water applications, such as oil-field engineering or cable and pipeline management. Recovering objects from great depths, while maintaining archaeological control over data, can be more challenging than recovering objects from shallow-water or terrestrial sites. The recording and documenting of the archaeology relied heavily on electronic and other technological equipment and systems.

The archaeological aim of the project was to identify and record the archaeological features of the shipwreck site and also to conduct experimental marine archaeology, seeking to combine present techniques and methodology with current deep-water ROV technology and equipment. In this investigation, new techniques and methods were developed that should prove useful for the emerging discipline of deep-water archaeology.

The wreck of the SS *Republic* lies oriented in a south-east to north-west line in the waters of the Gulf Stream. Including the debris field of artifacts that extends beyond the wreck itself, the area of the site that was investigated is 56,726 square meters. The site consists of a wreck lying relatively upright, with the two paddlewheels, port and starboard, both slightly canting outwards. The bow area is relatively flat (with no structures rising more than three or four feet from the seabed), showing evidence

Found lying on its portside, the SS Republic's rudder has been preserved by copper sheathing, installed over a century ago for protection.

that the vessel most likely landed on the seabed on her starboard bow. Both of the two bow anchors are lying upright on the seabed, with the anchor winch lying upright to starboard. The walking-beam engine is fairly intact and upright; it stands 4 meters (13 feet) high. Both of the boilers are displaced, shifted forward from their mountings, and are in a bad state of degradation. Most of the engine room has collapsed inward.

Large piles of coal, both forward and aft of the engine room, have spilled into the cargo holds. The stern area has collapsed, exposing the port lower hull and the keel. The rudder is lying on its port side, with a break along the top section at the gudgeon and pintle (these terms refer to the top hinge that fixes the rudder to the stern post). Beyond the wreck site, both to port and starboard, are pieces of the ship's hull and structures that have broken off during the wreck-formation process.

"Wreck formation" refers to an ongoing process of constant change, from the time the wreck occurred to the present, during which the site is affected by varied factors to reach its current state.

Much of the cargo was found lying scattered on top of and throughout the coal piles, both forward and aft. Most of the crates had been broken, with their contents now visible. The debris field around the wreck consisted of piles of slates, thousands of bottles, ceramics, and other cargo most likely moved there by the currents or displaced from the cargo holds during the sinking and wreck-formation processes.

Importantly, the distribution of the bottles and other artifacts found on the site aided the archaeological interpretation of the shipwreck processes, matching the historic accounts of the sinking. Survivor reports describe how the passengers and crew threw some of the cargo overboard before the ship finally sank, attempting to keep the ship afloat. As the vessel was sinking, its cargo holds were probably left open, allowing for some crates and their contents to wash out of the ship and to end up in a debris field adjacent to the shipwreck site. During the initial site-formation process, the strong currents may have caused certain categories of artifacts to be relocated downstream, away from their original shipboard positions.

Further, the archaeological investigation has shown that the wreck has been affected by the topography of the seabed, by exposure to the elements, and by accretion and scouring caused by the current and movement of sediments. Most of the wood has lost its strength, and the iron has been subject to marine environmental corrosion. Water, temperature, salinity, acidity, and marine biological activity are other considerations that may have affected the site.

Applying current marine archaeological techniques and marrying them with present systems used in commercial deep-water operations has yielded successful results. The recovery of the SS *Republic* has been groundbreaking in developing and testing new systems, in exploring and refining the methods and techniques needed to investigate deep-water wrecks.

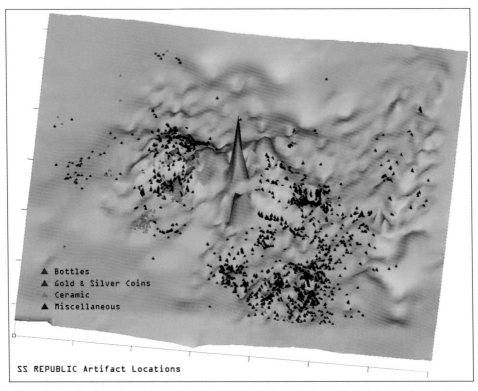

SS REPUBLIC Artifact Locations

This bathymetric (surface) chart shows the different types of artifacts plotted on a three-dimensional map of the SS Republic wreck site. The blue triangles represent the bottles scattered within the wreck site and in the debris field. The tall spike in the center is the ship's walking-beam engine. The two paddlewheels can also be seen on either side of the walking beam.

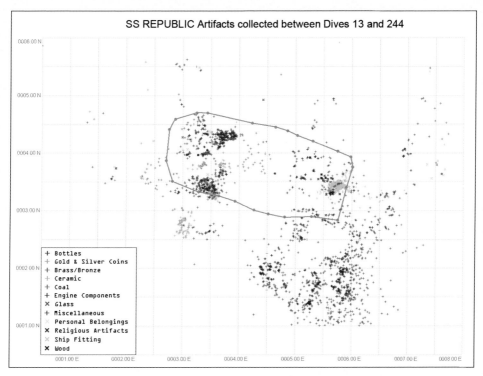

SS REPUBLIC Artifacts collected between Dives 13 and 244

Legend:
+ Bottles
+ Gold & Silver Coins
+ Brass/Bronze
+ Ceramic
+ Coal
+ Engine Components
× Glass
+ Miscellaneous
× Personal Belongings
× Religious Artifacts
× Ship Fitting
× Wood

The gray solid outline on this artifact distribution map shows the SS Republic, with the ship's bow at the left and its stern to the right. The blue crosses represent bottles scattered within the wreck site and in the debris field beyond the perimeter of the shipwreck. The large quantity of bottles to the lower right, outside the Republic, were probably moved there by the currents or displaced from the cargo hold during the sinking and wreck-formation processes. The distribution of the bottles aided the archaeological interpretation of the shipwreck site.

APPENDIX B

Resources

Books

American Bottles & Flasks and Their Ancestry, by Helen McKearin & Kenneth M. Wilson (Crown, 1978)

The Bertrand Bottles: A Study of 19th-century Glass and Ceramic Containers, by Ronald R. Switzer (National Park Service, 1974)

Bitters Bottles, by Carlyn Ring & William C. Ham (W. C. Ham/ Boyertown Publishing Co., 1998)

The Bottle Book: A Comprehensive Guide to Historic, Embossed Medicine Bottles, by Richard E. Fike (Peregrine Smith Books, 1987)

The Golden Age of Quackery, by Stewart H. Holbrook (Macmillan, 1959)

Hair Raising Stories, by Don Fadely (privately published, 1992)

The Illustrated Guide to Collecting Bottles, by Cecil Munsey (Hawthorn Books, 1970)

Nostrums and Quackery (American Medical Assn. Press, 1912)

The Toadstool Millionaire: A Social History of Patent Medicines in America before Federal Regulation, by James Harvey Young (Princeton University Press, 1961)

A Treasury of American Bottles, by William C. Ketchum, Jr. (Bobbs-Merrill, 1975)

Websites

http://www.bottlebooks.com (Digger Odell Publications)

http://www.worldlynx.net/sodasandbeers/ shapes.htm (Antique Soda & Beer Bottles)

http://www.blm.gov/historic_bottles/ typing.htm (On Bottle Types, by U.S. Dept. of the Interior, Bureau of Land Management)

http://www.antiquebottles.com

MORE ABOUT ODYSSEY

The ocean floor, it is believed, may hold more than three million shipwrecks – an amazing cornucopia of cultural goods transported by mankind for more than 3,000 years. Until very recently, this astounding wealth has been virtually inaccessible. Deep-ocean pioneers Greg Stemm and John Morris embarked on a mission over twenty years ago to bring up these amazing historical treasures to the light of day.

Their company, Odyssey Marine Exploration, Inc., is unique in the world. It has brought together the talents of some of the world's most experienced technicians, archaeologists, and engineers, and with this expertise has discovered hundreds of wrecks: ancient Phoenician and Roman shipwrecks, 20th-century U-boats and passenger liners, airplanes spanning the age of aviation, and the Civil War-era sidewheel steamer SS *Republic*.

Odyssey's approach combines the latest in state-of-the-art technology with thorough research and a passion for nautical history and archaeology. Their database contains thousands of deep-ocean shipwrecks, each featuring its own intriguing story and, in many cases, valuable and fascinating cargoes.

Odyssey believes that with these discoveries comes a responsibility to share with the public the knowledge gained from these expeditions. This book provides a glimpse of what can be learned from one category of artifact from one unique shipwreck: the bottles from the SS *Republic*.

The Odyssey team invites you to follow their progress as new shipwrecks are discovered and new tales are told by long-lost ships spanning thousands of years of mankind's history.

Please visit the company's website at www.shipwreck.net and discover a whole new world of deep-ocean exploration.

Index